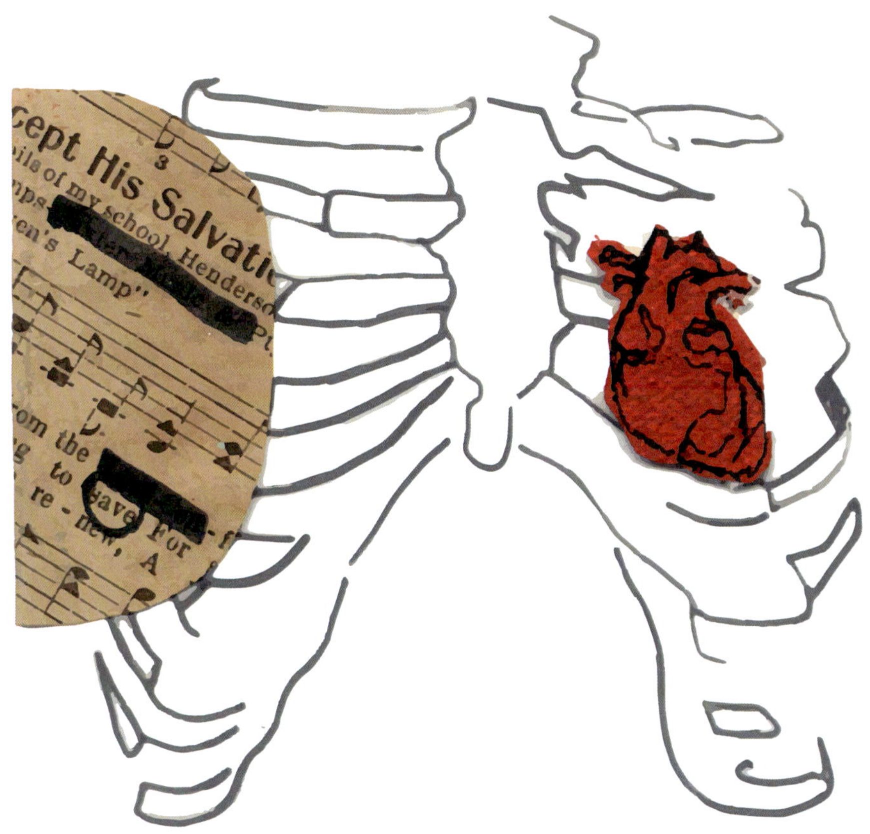
cept His Salvati
ils of my school, Henders
en's Lamp"
om the
g to
re - new, A

AF584625

DIG

BRYAN BORLAND

stillhouse
press
CRAFT PUBLISHING FOR ARDENT SPIRITS

FAIRFAX, VIRGINIA

First Edition

All inquiries may be directed to:

Stillhouse Press
4400 University Drive, 3E4
Fairfax, VA 22030
www.stillhousepress.org

Library of Congress Control Number: 2016935266

ISBN-10: 0-9905169-8-9
ISBN-13: 978-0-9905169-8-9

Art: Jonathan Kent Adams
Art Direction & Cover Design: Douglas J. Luman
Interior Design: Kady Dennell

Printed in the United States of America by McNaughton & Gunn

This publisher is a proud member of

[clmp]

I felt these were messages left along the trail for me

– Adrienne Rich,
from her essay, "The Rotted Names"

—

For Seth

CONTENTS

DIG

DIG

You want the dirt,
all the sin and tendon
you think are under these nails. I beg,
instead, forget ten years of my life.
Let's redact the documents, change
the sheets on the bed. Draw lines
through names and dates. Relationships
are never linear. Let's start, if we must
start, at the last end we know, the slime
of those boys we buried in the yard. Or start
the story in our middle, with two dogs
pulling us down this path, far enough along to
know we survive. Deep enough that
questions turn to statements.
What is a poet? What is a husband?
Forget there was a time we didn't know
one another. Don't ask
about candles of ceremony. What meals
were eaten from these plates.
If you must remember something,
remember this: I am a poet.
You hear I was a husband.
Or some form of that word
before I was your husband.
You had lovers, too. We bring
ink to this, books from other tribes,
societies whose languages had
nothing of what we are together.

A FORM OF THAT WORD

WEATHER, THIS

Dear Bryan   the storm is soon
to begin   I write not in warning as you
will appreciate the autumn flowers
you always wanted   The herb garden   fragrant
basil and rosemary you think dead from drought
will come alive again in September
Instead I write to bolt down your bones
scarecrow they turn out to be   You already know
the direction of these winds   The strange
chill of a home in the beginning of wane
A week from now you will be tucked into bed
by a lover who will stab you in your sleep
You will swim in bloody pools
He will tell you dreams and poems mean nothing

Listen   dream this poem
How this rain will grow you
a family   How some part of you
remembers the hunger of time   smells
the blood   sees your prints in the mud   We are
powerless to what is by right of nature ours
these lunar pulls   these campfires warm   you night-
bathed when you'll swim together   two
untamable things in the breathing river   Your arms
will fold like paper birds around him   Your histories
will circle   starving beasts soon to eat   You'll make
shelter of every crater and scar   Every pain
a guide   Everything is instinct

THE BODY IS A DAMN HARD THING TO KILL

While I sleep beside him   the body is
in motion   I plead for quiet
The body is constantly talking back
I say *anniversary* and *ten years*
The body says *not yet*   When I find
comfort the body thirsts for
discomfort   The body grows
bored by its own heart so it becomes
the eater of hearts   I do not realize
until I taste the blood   Then I am faced
with two choices   compassion or rage
If compassion   the body becomes
a vehicle   I merge with the body
If rage   the body becomes an impossible
skill to master though
I will try   I will try by closing my eyes
but all I see is another body

CHEATED

How I didn't
follow him into the bathroom
go to him beyond the havoc
light of morning   allow my hand to
read the story beneath his waistband
make the first move   set the trap
pull my feet into his lap   let my venom
years fall at his bare toes as he stepped
locomotive from the shower all
power and steam to become
(myself) / (the villain) : *choose one*

I do not understand

How another man   my lover
did these things

How I wanted to do them too

MAD HOUSEWIFE

There were signs of his madness
He fell in love with the vomit he scrubbed
on the bathroom floor because
it came from a boy
It spilled into the front yard and there he sat
waiting   waiting for all to see
singing his lunatic songs
Neighbors said he went a little crazy
He said madness holds a beauty
He saw a bird in a stairwell
fluttering   fluttering its wings
against a glass wall   He found
this bird knew all his stories   He took
it in his hands   calmed it with
the darkness only his body could create
walked it to the sky   He's that kind
of man   Someone told it the darkest
parts of his story   The bird from its branch
sang along   His lunatic songs
His darkest parts   He's that kind
of man   The bird knows this
and still sings along

SLAUGHTER IN THREE PARTS

1

Halfway home the sky turns violent   I drive them
together   cannot see the road in front of me
It's my eyes that betray me   that after
such distance bleed for sleep
so I can dream these poems

2

He tells me dreams and poems mean nothing
But I do dream
of my lightning-rod spine
shattered by passing trains
In the refrigerator his food
rots to poison

3

I murder everything
pull honeysuckle from the ground
with angry hands   Call my mother
in tears   I am alone
when I wake to find them
watching television without me

SUMMERING WITH ANDY WARHOL

I'm not drinking and it feels
so great, you wrote on June 19, 1981.

It's June 19, 2014, and I suffer
no illusions about my relationship with alcohol,

though I have cut up my credit cards. *I've got to*
try to stop taking Valium, you wrote. I've got to stop

fantasizing about group sex. We are 33
years to the day apart, each

steeling our resolves through the lines
in our journals, a rare moment of

clarity and a list to
make us live longer. You won't

have a drink for two months. For your birthday
you'll receive 500 carats of pulverized jewels.

You'll nurse a champagne headache and
scribble how diamond dust can kill, how it's

a good way to murder someone with beauty.
I'll call Citibank and order a replacement card.

Pour a martini and put out snacks for the orgy
of reading piled on the coffee table. Summer

wasn't meant for resolutions. We fail
spectacularly, don't we Andy?

WALKING THROUGH FIELDS OF RUIN

Eric sends me a friend request after
his parole. He starts calling.
Sixteen. Seventeen times in a row.
When I do not answer, he leaves me
messages saying *I have to talk to you;*
I have to see you. There is the madness
in his voice that comes from needing
something forbidden. In the middle
of the night, he sends a text:
Come sneak me out. He means
from the halfway house. He is an addict;
I am methamphetamine.

Michael cannot spell.
His status updates are simple. They reek
of cold beer, deer meat, straight man.
The smell of bachelorhood.
Where is the confident boy
with the balls to place his hand
on my school-bus-riding leg?
I know what you are, he said then.
Now he announces to the world:
99% DNA match. Guess I'm a daddy.

Joshua does not confirm me,
does not confirm he was my first.
He does not confirm how he
would touch me underneath
the blanket, how I would touch
him, how he wrote me love
letters from Joplin, Missouri. Yesterday
a tornado ate the heart
of the town. Now Joplin
is gone. Now so is he.

THE KITCHEN TABLE TREATY

If this is meant to survive
we must agree now on the terms
of war   itself a contradiction as
war by definition tramples lines

Do not say tonight there will be
no war   you know armies
gather in all backyards   everything
we read can turn against us   the poison
ivy you cut from the fence weeks ago
remains in skeleton vines to crawl again

We have to have these conversations
we are not the enemy   never
with words as weapons across
the table   instead we map the battle
inward   days when one or both of us
carries the madness of the other
like a wounded soldier slung across the back

And believe me now   there will be madness
when we have promised to end these bodies looking
lived in   so at times our breaths
will smell of the adolescent
dank and semen
the swamps we wade through
when absence makes us not ourselves

You are not yourself
today   so I am not myself
but tonight we again will be
ourselves   this is
the treaty of attraction
blood from the wrist of marriage
we are human countries   you and I
the rules of war between us this:
let's just hold
each other tonight ok?
All night.
No sleep.

THREE WAYS TO MEAN IT

(1) *Dig* your nails into the armrest of the airplane.
Dig your fingers into the pulpy flesh of the orange.
Dig yourself into another body beyond the burnt
peeling of the skin. Dig down into summer.
Dig down deep.

Dig down into the bruised
meat of your own back. Into the hurt
and joy, but push. Dig inside yourself. Mine
yourself for the world beneath the world. The god
beneath the talk of god.

Dig because you like him.
Dig because you love him.
Dig because you (2) *dig* him. Let that
meaning overtake
this mess.

Here are the rules. Do not take unnecessary shots.
Do not throw sucker punches or heirloom lamps
or meaningless jewelry out the window of a moving car.
Do not take (3) *digs* at anyone whose imperfection turns
you to yourself. This includes yourself.

Dig. Say it with me.
Dig as challenge. Dig as miracle of destruction.
Dig as science of creation. Say the word then
dig deeper. Do not be afraid. Say the word.

HOW IT ENDS

I pack his things carefully at first,
fold his clothes like a flag fresh off a coffin.
I let this delicate touch be a last act of love
until the mismatch of their hands appears
so I give myself a gift to get through the night:
for once forget the reigning rule
of craft and let the cliché of throwing
his clothes on the lawn remain.
I master my arson.
I let those clothes burn.
I learn there are no clean breaks.
I cry. I cry to my aunt in Montana.
My therapist in her office. My author
under contract in our second business meeting.
I cry for my father. Tell the empty chairs I miss him.
Cry even harder when the radio cries back.
I feel more betrayed by the house than by he who betrays me,
the walls that watched the dismantling of a family,
the carving of our story in another man's thigh.
I hear a ticking in my chest I think is a bomb.
When it blows the living room teaches me
the terrible scream of a space dissected.
A body post-dying, the house
feels betrayed by me too.

THESE BOYS

THE JUMPERS

A thousand boys move to San Francisco
where history hits like water. The body stops. Just
like the jumpers the heart keeps going. Some boys travel
there to launch themselves from bridges, all scraped-
knee red, circus angels doing backflips with needles jutting
from naked bellies. Hear them sing till waves eat their bones.
Pass them down Chinatown's vibrant rows, headless
chickens hanging like wasted rich kids from chandeliers.
Some boys want to fly before they want to write. They kiss
the feet of pretty ones, don't speak to men making love
where mapmakers pissed themselves and left beautiful
stains. Some boys find jobs and apartments by reading
obituaries. The jobs are crushing, the apartments' empty
bedrooms full of mirrors. These boys jump to die. Other boys
find jobs and apartments by reading the pages of stolen
library books. The real jobs begin at quitting time.
They smile in photographs. They are not victims
of geography, these boys. These boys, they jump to live.

THE SIGNIFICANCE OF MATTHEW

Afterwards, in the community theater circuit,
drama boys put on his shoes then disappeared
into pieces the audience took home. I think
it was the first time my mother really saw
summer's sudden turn to autumn in the west,
a place she'd never been, or how the skin
of brittle leaves can be moved by rivers all
across this country. What does it mean to be
a giant in the weeds, a stone for a forced decision?
What does it do to a spirit when the broken shell
it leaves behind makes the living human? Enough
falls have passed that now I see what she
stood to lose. When Matthew was murdered,
my mother couldn't forget his face.
When Matthew was murdered, the fence-
sitters had to choose.

THESE BOYS

Olive Handkerchief

Carson and Sullivan, they passed around pictures
of their women back home, flesh in the hairy palms
of soldiers who compared breasts and cracked jokes.
Sully's corn-fed girl won by consensus of the boys.
Red-faced Andrews stomped to the barracks
suddenly protective of his girlfriend's flat chest.
Our eyes met till his retreated, green
like those of my Nebraska man. I miss him
with the intensity of war, with the pain
of a jaw blown away or severed vocal chords,
unable to speak to the men who hold
my bloody heart in their hands, my brothers
with whom I share more intimacy
than a sexual act. We cheat death together,
dodge its horny hands and guide
its heat onto other unfortunate souls.
We are uniform: eat, sleep, piss, die,
but no one ever asks the question,
no one ever grabs his photo and
wonders who has the bigger dick.

Aqua Handkerchief

I almost drowned in the Colorado River
when I was thirteen. I'd gone to summer camp

with my neighbor, Randy, because I
wanted to kiss him. I'd gone rafting

to impress him. I was terrified.
I could barely swim.

We lost control and I flipped backwards
and fell into the rapids.

I breathed the water. I swallowed the river.
I swallowed the merboys that leapt through the current.

I fought until the end of time.
I fought until my body went limp.

When I awoke, I was on the bank, my legs
still submerged, my back flat against the sand.

Randy was over me. Randy was kissing me.
Randy was crying. Randy was touching me.

When I coughed, Randy smiled.
Randy hugged me.

I think of him every time I kiss a man
in the Colorado River.

Gold Handkerchief

Third grade was the year I picked up
cusses easy like winter colds and asked my parents
what *masturbation* meant. It was the year we found
a video in the park labeled *Pumping Irene*,
exposed tape spiraling out of its plastic casing
like guts from a stab wound. We fancied ourselves
healers, laying dirty hands on her pure body
in selfish acts of resuscitation. When that failed,
we were left to imagine the body of a woman
and the things adults did beyond the gravity
and pull of our eight-year-old minds. We were
scab-hearted boys chattering with newfound
vocabulary, using the bluntest words for anatomy
like Christmas toys. My friends pictured Irene
as a busty blonde, nothing like our mothers
or sisters, while my thoughts circled the men
I knew would resemble American Gladiators,
the ones who would lift Irene over their heads,
their deltoid muscles worthy of gold.

White Handkerchief

Seventeen boys sleep between us
in a crowded bed, a paranormal orgy
of recall, ghosts of lovers still living
or dead. I think of the one struck
by lightning on his grandfather's farm,
of how, if his cock had been in my mouth,
I would have been electrocuted.
Another fucked his brain with a bullet
and was found by his younger brother.
I'd had them both and remember
how their toes curled the same when they came.
There are happier endings, some
with wives and children, one
with a song on the radio. Every autumn
I think of how his hair smelled like burning leaves.
They're all here, even though they're not,
even though they're long gone
and we sleep content, our arms intertwined,
his old flames, too, leaking into his dreams,
puddles of memory that never quite evaporate.

DON'T KILL THE DEAD

I'm learning not to kill
the dead in every poem. I've written poems about
my brother's death, an entire book about my father's
death and some days must talk myself
down from the ledge of repetition.
Some days I dam the walls. Some days I
damn the walls and jump into things
I've newly noticed, like how my fluency in
the common language of ghosts has eroded
over time. I rarely dream of them.
When I do, they are background noise,
not the loud songs of myself I heard
as a younger man. The long dead, I'm learning,
become quiet with age. My brother never made it
to this second puberty of silver hair. In my mind
he's a mixture of space and light.
My father doesn't answer when I ask him
how a heart is designed to pump through pain.
He doesn't know. Now
his throat is full of rocks. We're designed
to disappear like this, piece by piece,
the same as our bodies begin to fail
if we make it past a certain point. I'm aging.
The arch of my foot is sore today. I feel
my hinges when I stand. I cannot remember
my brother's voice. The poetry of it
abandons me.

DIVE

More hotels have gone up in this city. They line
the sidewalks like bored policemen keeping
the crowds dumb. You want to know why
none of them have dive bars off their
lobbies instead of stools wiped clean after
every ass. You want to know why we
still live here when every other kingdom calls.
We walk until we find two beers under a tin roof
and splinters in our elbows. It's a hundred degrees
out. It feels like a hundred ten. It's not yet the end
of July and we had to get out of that old house to
escape the heat before we stripped naked and
pressed our bodies to the hardwood like animals.
We wear only what we have to today, ragged
old shirts and shorts that show we're
interested in being men. I used to be embarrassed
by my nothing shoulders and below them
a chest that blossomed barbed wire too early.
Isn't it funny how we run from things that make us
beautiful? Once I wanted smooth skin
and everything clean. Now I want the hair
of dark places. I want to drink these beers
to cool us off then screw when we're buzzed
on a bed that's scratched and clawed but has
never seen a better day than this.

LONOKE

We both come to this having lived
here all our lives. Only now do we see how breathing

things drop from trees. Mid-afternoon the insects
have white wings, our backyard full of moons.

Last week a ballet of sunset moved into night. Everything
a show. Even your shape is foreign to your eyes.

The V of your abdomen. The rise of your shoulders.
Your muscles reach for me like begonias reach for light.

We've found one another grown in this
half-mowed cemetery grass.

Across the highway are adolescent fields,
bodies on the cusp of gin.

I am the son of a farmer.
You are the son of a mortician.

We grieve like we eat like we kiss
these lantern ways of our American south.

Small towns have their limits. Cars filled
with families pass. Seeing us they think they

understand why I cling to you.
Something has died.

Yes. We buried our dead today.
Now we celebrate our living.

SLEDGEHAMMER

February. You sit alone in the parking lot
of a church before a reading. Your partner
of ten years sleeps at home. You've come alone again
and here are the nerves. You open the door, flip
the switch, fake smile. You are lucky to have practiced
this act before. Nod to Preacher, Brother Kevin.
You keep repeating: *God is love.*
                                        God is love.
                                                        God is love.
You enter the room. The strange familiar. He
is the youngest, sitting with his sister. He is
the anticipation of a second kiss. The knowledge
of hunger in another mouth.

March is a sick lion. You've not dressed for this:
the cold of anonymous love and a cough
you can't shake, so you daydream. Golden
Gate Bridge. Six Gallery, where Ginsberg
thought of his brother and read "Howl"
for the first time. You've kept the boy's name
on the torn page of a Bible. You cannot bring
yourself to throw this holy thing away.

April doesn't bring rain, not like it should,
as if lightning and thunder, downpours and spring storms
are reserved for love and pain of summer, as if the grass,
teased only with dew, is lucky in its brittle, thirsty green,
in its slow fade to washed-out gold, then brown.
You find a poem he wrote. A transaction of energy.
A negotiated exchange. His voice to whoever
is listening over the industrial static and right
now, that's you.

May ends in beginnings. Another parking lot, more nerves,
Brother, do you have a dollar? asks a man on the street.
The lightning of empathy hits so you give three.
You're here to meet him. To hammer out some heaven
of work. It's the simple, brilliant tussle of an idea,
the smile imprinted, his glasses, your prayers to his torso.
You know he spends his days at the college but this is more

lust than lecture, more temple than classroom.
You have things to teach him. You have things to learn.

June is three decades long. You fall this month,
that lucky accident of arms and ass,
blue shorts you lend that fit. You brother him,
tell him so while every pulse through vein and brain aches
for more. You see a band ask *Are You Lightning?*
You know the answer. You swallow beer, drive home,
wipe vomit, love vomit because it came from him.

July is when the gods turn angry.
You allow yourself only a breath
of his curly hair. There is not enough
air. You make ambulance of his eyes.
You think yourself lucky. You swim together.
He climbs on to you. You stiffen, swallow, love
hard. You put your hands on his shoulders, hold him.
You call him brother when, really, you want to kiss him.

August. You've been with a man for nearly ten years.
You've never fallen full body into the wet mouth
of another poet. And now there are books to sell, and now
there's a publishing company when there wasn't before.
You fall in love with poetry and the man falls out of love with you.
Poetry becomes a boy you meet who shows you your teachers
were wrong, and your preachers, your men. Your employers
and politicians. It is everything they fear. What's denied
in themselves. They are scared of this, of you learning this.
Of the power between these poems and you.

GOLD AND SILVER MIXED TO ONE

There is a visiting poet at the lectern who
fumbles with her glasses, forgets

they are on her head, or on her nose,
who loses her book and her place, who stops mid-

poem to explain that Bruges is a city in Belgium or
how Friesian is a breed of horse or when she's written

a lie in a line or why it's a writer's responsibility
to record anything that deserves to be remembered.

Or, that the love of her life, the poet to whom
she was married for 25 years, died in his sleep last June.

At the post-reading dinner she requests that
Seth and I sit on either side of her. She shows

us their two rings she now wears on one hand, one
gold and one silver, like ours. She lets me hold them.

She orders for us, vodka rocks with lemon and lime.
She says without him, she's lost

her first reader. Without him, she never
knows if what she's written is any good.

THE DUANE EFFECT

I buy purple shoes. Duane says
they go with nothing so they go with everything.
The right and the left are different sizes. Duane
talks the clerk into giving me a discount.
At the next store I buy a turquoise
jacket. Duane says it's mint. He tells me
he makes shopping more economical
by swapping price tags from cheaper pieces.
He's developed a technique. Which means
someone someday will pay more for less. I tell him
I worry he'll be punched in the face by a stranger.
He responds by asking a stranger if she likes
to dance. The stranger likes to dance. Duane looks
back at me as if this will save him. It probably will.
Duane lives with a gay couple. I avoid
more shopping by stealing their shirts.
Duane is this type of influence. He tells me
to take one shirt but I take two. I feel like
Duane will appreciate this. I've never met
his roommates. They're traveling when we visit.
My husband and I sleep in their bed. My husband
is my husband because of Duane. Duane sent us
into marriage to queer it from the inside. My husband
and I fuck in Duane's roommates' bed. I press
the underwear I find in the room to my
husband's face. I don't know whose they are.
We use their lube, too. We do not use their edible body paint.
We cum in their towels and pet their dog. We score free
whiskey at the Eagle by wearing stolen jock straps.
Duane is this type of influence. He rents a locker
to house our pants for a quarter.
I keep the purple shoes on.
Duane is right. They go with everything.

PENANCE

Certain sins can be beautiful. I'm thinking
of greed, this hungry want of you, of every foot of dirt.
I tell our friends how I've allowed myself to become
dependent. How the welding of my needs to your hips goes
against everything I before believed. We're taught
to love only so much until we hold something
back for the inevitable days when the birds fall
from the sky and we bleed from behind. That happens,
I suppose, and who knows how we'll change
by the time it's our decade in these books. The truth is
your dirt does not scare me. I want it all. This
is no time for mercy.

PERILUNE

Wulf the mystic tells us not to place weight on herds
of symbols   spit on cave walls   scratches in buffalo

skin that spell our names   says they are everywhere
we look once we learn how to see   in every city we visit

there's us   remember the photograph of the sisters
our faces   *were we Crow*   the twin eyes of Chicago brothers

the oldest boy's knuckles bleeding affection   the letters
l o v e   on each of four knuckles   we write

gentle postcards for our future selves to find   frontiers-
men of dusty west   wanderers of northern brick   do you

remember how many times we have failed   we try
again until we get it right   in the easy wild

of these shared sheets   we learn to read
the sky   how the patterns of stars repeat   I follow the curve

of your belly   you touch the freckle on my right ear
we are growing accustomed to this repetition

we are growing a
custom to this repetition.

HUMAN RESOURCES

There is a day job
forty hours of contusion
In my bag I carry the poems of radicals
yet from my desk I choose which
minimum wage worker
urinates in a cup

I hear the song of that worker
in my sleep

Below my walls
mothers are paid 7.50 an hour
I make more than three times that to
fight their unemployment benefits when
they are fired for being late again
because their daughters' stomachs
turn inward

What sins can the body allow
If I took them myself I'd fail
every test I give
I hear the song of the worker
in my sleep   What troubles
can be justified
when I am soft in my tyranny
when I say I'm just
doing my job
when I allow my body

this sin

COMMUNION

Over coffee Adrienne says the people she can trust are the ones
who will let her have her death. Are we keeping her

too long? Better a literary journal than a shopping mall, she says.
I don't pretend to understand her shadow puppetry

against these tables for two. Klein played poet at her feet and even he
doesn't answer direct when asked what she'd think of these lines. Mostly

we're the hungry content in our conversation. She at least humors us
when we tell of old friends not congratulating the marriage. She says

they're mere actors who want us to stay and further the plot. I ask if my
notebook is a script I've tied to her hands, if I've any real claim to her

possibility. She laughs and says of course. She reminds us of her
highway séances with Wallace Stevens. How

she'd turn left where his ghost finger pointed and end up God
knows where.

NEW DRUG

The chemistry of ethics I don't know. I ask
the doctor for the pill. His degree of separation:
our state is a city, our city is a town. His wife
isn't queer. From his box he talks down.

The monogamy of this physician-patient
relationship strains. The monotony of these
conversations. How my tests
are meant for someone else. How I beg for
blood in vial, not cholesterol, you fuck.
How I beg for an extra layer of cloth.

The ethics of marriage I know. Be good
to yourself. Your body. Our body.
His body.

The judgment: I say it plain. We fuck some.
We make love more.
These are two different things. We come
from a long line of great vanishing. This
anthology is strong. I tell him the names.
Reginald. Paul. Essex. Leon down
the lane. My people. There are no mistakes.

I say it plain. Write my name.
I love. I fuck, or I don't.
I'm good until I'm not.
There are hollow places in us
that are hungry. We know the risk
of not having them filled.

COMPANY MEETING

You revise in the study.
Around the corner I sit in the orange chair
brought from your mother's home and read
American Poet, sticky with peach jam from
yesterday's breakfast, Merwin's "The Room"
clinging to "For the Anniversary of My Death."
Our dog sleeps exactly between us, lulled by
the usual sounds, clicking keys, turning pages.

There is work and there is life.

This is life.

Forget that it doesn't pay the bills.
Forget the deadlines and false crowns
and gossip of worthy heirs. There is no
kingdom beyond this yellow house.
There is no throne. There is our bed.
We are indebted to no iron-clad contract
more than the one signed in the humidity of
our own sweat. At this point there is no separation
between us. Love a man and love all he becomes,
however he evolves, whatever grows
on the plant of his skin.

Here is what I would say
if I owed it enough to be said.
The book I write or do not write
you memorize, as I memorize the book
you write or do not write.
These are the books of us.
Even if no lines are ever written.
Even if we forget how to read or be read.

SANTA MONICA WITHOUT YOU

Last night on the pier I watched the sunset.

You handed it to me from the east.

I handed it to someone on the other side of the ocean.

I don't know who I handed it to.

Walking alone in the sand felt like cheating.

Another man's hand doesn't feel like cheating.

Twice last week the question. Are you open?

Twice last week the answer in too many words.

Yes.

And no.

And yes.

It's easy for me to accept the smell of foreign beds on your body.

It's impossible for me to accept the salt of Santa Monica on mine.

BLOOD IN THE THROAT

HOW IT BEGINS

That first single morning I'll cut the grass with my teeth in the evening I'll run half-naked and mad in the heat leap over the veins of the pavement in time with the shoeless runner ahead of me just to feel connected to someone // I won't eat for a week so when Friday comes I'll go alone to the restaurant order ribs chew the bones clean I'll wipe my hands when he phones saying he'll pick me up and take me to the dive bar where he'll keep calling me baby by mistake on what won't be a date we'll swoon in other people's smoke we'll listen to dead bands play my leg will always press too hard against his leg so hard it's like we'll need each other to stand at all.

YOU, HOUSE MARTIN

Sweetheart we've landed
on a new planet   advice column said
never become complacent
so one Sunday after breakfast in a walk in the rain
I said let's move   you said let's move
by the next Sunday we had numbers
on Martin Street
worried the renter so much his hair
fell out and we fell in.

Sometimes it feels we're boys
in the trees or playing house
where we take turns being wives
for booze at five or one husband
sending the other out the door
and down the steps with a kiss and
the trail of ants in the morning.

There are things we allow from an old house
a leaky faucet   dents in the walls from
the angry years of 1939 or 1957
the light in the kitchen that has no switch
the air is different on Martin Street
the gas stove and her mothering clicks
the bumpers of cars blue and hip
a mix of age these neighbor women
who knew the pantry was full of moths.

Once we were new   now we are
ourselves on Martin Street   we
itch and kiss   we
check the lease for some unknown date
we've our own marks to leave
our grease in the oven   handprint on thigh
your fingernails against these walls
my fingernails against these walls.

EAT THE WHOLE WORLD

Thom Gunn says we should box up our books and move
to California. He says this on a sunny Arkansas morning
when we get funny looks from people in the diner
at our table for three. *Honey* is the waitress's favorite word.
She spills water on the *Collected* between us. Here the coffee
is weak. Poetry is foreign and walled away. Forced
recitation. Selected Dickinson but barely a taste.
Pop quizzes kill any hope these children will make it
to the man who pushes us west. Thom orders nothing.
Sings of North Beach breakfasts and Caffè Trieste.
Says you can still get by cheap if you have a poet's heart
and an angel's ass. That it's all in reach: the Public Library,
a New Year's Eve in the Embarcadero, a thrift store
in the Mission that sells more Ashbery than tight pairs of pants.
He tells us not to narrow our dreams. Wants to show us
the Haight, the Bay ferry. Hums how he swam the Atlantic.
What's two thousand miles? We have every reason to stay.
We have every reason to go. And Thom? He just smiles.

THE WAITER, THE REVOLUTIONARY, THE LEGISLATOR, & THE POET

The waiter who poured the coffee last night
takes the palace this morning. And you

are not in a motel room in Tempe writing of
how the mask he wears makes his eyes

look human. Or asking who will watch
the children as their mothers are turned

away from a lunch counter in Phoenix sixty years
after the south carved the same harsh lessons

into the bark of its pine. The past is repeating
itself, Adrienne, so when will you rise again in

these crowds of characters, the colleges
and professors, the gas station clerks, the old

poets who all know history well but remain
absent in cold capitals where

laws are being constructed, revised, and
pounded into form. Today

the world needs another love poem
like it needs blood in the throat.

A JUNE WEDDING (WITH DISTANCE)

In Koreatown last night
my accent was a disguise.
The British woman who asked me
to dance said it was her birthday.
It wasn't her birthday.
She wasn't British.
Her accent told her secrets.
The yellow bandana in my pocket told mine.
I sang "Thunder Road" and
got back to my room too late to call.
You got out of bed too early to call.
I'm hungover and don't want to see the photos.

Tomorrow the police helicopter will not circle overhead.
I'll go for a run for the first time in a week.
The Supreme Court will make our marriage
as real as our parents' marriages
were and I'll feed the finches bits of pancake.

I'll cry with Emily at breakfast.
I'll cry when I run alone though Los Angeles.
I'll cry when the barista
calls me her *corazón*.

HIS DOG

You've taken the dog for a walk
From inside I hear commotion on the street
I see two bulldogs on your heels
You frantic and powerless
release the leash so he can run
but he is caught and I do what I'm not
supposed to do   what I have to do
to save him   reach in with both hands
and prove myself strong enough for you
to always know how dangerous
I love you

FRIENDS ASK US HOW WE KNOW THIS MARRIAGE IS RIGHT

and we tell them we just know.
The real answer, though,

is in how I once had a fear of meeting a man
who never knew my father. In how, since we married,

I've felt him less or maybe if I'm brave I'll admit
not at all. It's in the poem we found in our

first month that spoke of the dark horse
and the dead rider and the lines

I have brought him to you
I have done all I can.

LOOK ALIVE, KID

Breathing is an act of
war or joy or sabotage or life. You choose
indifference which carries with it the sting
of privilege. The boys you bed might fill
a first collection. The parties might
fill a second. You might say *I don't*
write political poems. The icons
in your autograph book might write your name
prettier than you ever could. Wild
fields of technology weren't sown
to weather jail cells or genocide. Begging
for fame will eventually turn your hands or
face to casualty of stone. Do not smile
long enough in snapshots and you'll forget
the purpose of your mouth. But you
can't know this. Not yet.

EASTER IN YOUR HOMETOWN

I've married into religion, mothered
by your Pentecostal ma who calls us *the boys,*

who prayed so hard for a son she made a god
who made you. We know there will be gossip

between the pews. You straighten my tie.
She no longer cooks breakfast for your father

who lives in the rental house across town.
We wipe the dirt from her good church shoes

the morning after your brother sleeps on the couch
so we can share his bed in your old room.

After the service, she asks my birthday,
writes it on the calendar nailed to the kitchen wall.

This is resurrection, I know. The end of one
faith. The beginning of another.

YOUR OLDER BROTHER GIVES ME MY NAME

At your father's wedding
we stand exposed as rusted nails
as I'm introduced again and again as *Bryan*

just *Bryan*

no context

no *Seth's husband*

just *Bryan*

until your older brother sees the puzzled looks

the stubborn aunts

the woman who wanders in
from the street for cake

the whispers and questions and finally

the rescue

he's not a cousin

they look at him

he's my brother-in law.

MIRROR BOYS

My husband thinks of his own father's chest
of knowledge and worries he doesn't have the tools to
build a son into being. But I have seen his hands pull
beauty from the barren, roses and stray dogs brought
back to life by the gentle rains from his brow. I know
some day he will make our boy smile by telling of how,
before the animals ever dreamed him, we chose
clothes for his unborn body in a department store
or of the afternoon in the water park when we
pointed at families swimming and invented his knees.
I remember our flight from Boston through a storm,
how he held my hand and asked about my childhood to grant
my mind clemency from the rocking cabin. We were still
stubborn then, getting to know each other, embarrassed
to show the other a single flaw. After an emergency
landing in Texas, I refused to get on another plane and
rented a car to drive the five hours home. He promised to stay
awake next to me but fell asleep against the passing fields,
exhausted from keeping a hundred-ton machine in the air
through will and love for me. My husband worries he will not be
a good father. I fear turbulence and runway fires, everything
that could go wrong. I do not fear nights when our son will cry.
I've heard the songs my husband will sing. I rest easy.

SATELLITE PASSING OVERHEAD

Just as you are setting the table
I pull you from the house into the belly
of the front yard to see the satellite pass
the same way husbands have pulled wives
and wives have pulled wives and husbands
have pulled husbands away from the dinner
table and into the night for years to see
these things only in the light of the dark
there are so many pieces of the sky
moving so many birds as stars or stars
as birds such a flock of space matter
a pack of meteors we can't tell
which is the satellite and which is
every other possibility we dream together
Somewhere there is a man
missing this missing what's passing right
overhead standing in a meeting room
in a small town asking how many
believe in keeping us out of this tradition
My husband pulls me inside after the
sky becomes still again telling me
C'mon the food's getting cold
Somewhere a man is missing this

I'LL TELL YOUR LITTLE BROTHER YEARS FROM NOW

of how, at four AM in our office,
after the carpet has burned itself down

to the scorched earth of red patches on your back
and my knees, I am falling asleep again

and hear his name rise from your mouth like a spirit.
Of how, as our chests slow their bite and tear

in the babyteeth between night and morning,
you wonder if he knows how much you love him.

I'll tell him of how you wore your father's shirts
and gassed up the mower, wanting instead to teach

his fingers to make sounds that stay on his bones
better than the hand-me-down cardigans his body rejects.

I will tell him of how your worry is thick with the smoke
of a house fire, of the fine line between warmth

and blister. Of how you go back in to find him
and almost come out, every time, melted together.

MY CAT

We pray all night for the cat's death
before morning but when you wake
he is waiting for you in the kitchen
unable to walk but still driven by a hunger
for food he cannot hold
It's true what my mother says
that when it's time you know
and I know but I cannot
heat the towel like you do
cannot gently place him in the crate
cannot take him to the vet
Instead I kiss you both
goodbye and drive to work

AT A BACH CONCERT

1

It's dark and we are buzzing fireflies after the reading, on
Boylston laughing in the white laps of old churches
like we're snow angels free from the frozen earth,
our socks wet, our coats too thin, unused to being buttoned
and zipped in our southern versions of winter, unused to
but right at home on this fantastic, foreign street of tonic
and spirit, where one month / one week / two days from now
there will be ash and burn at the finish of the marathon,
but tonight is the night before the morning I will marry him
and all I can think of is *life*.

2

The book of Adam says is it not good for man to be alone,
but I have guarded my solitude, waiting for this boy with copper
head of hair wrapped around my ribs before the world gave him
a name. I swear to God I felt the ground howl the moment he
passed into this place, my desert years spent waiting beneath
a sky streaked with whatever lifetimes came before, whatever
stories they'll tell of us after. I am mixing my religions, I know,
our spiritual lives as much a patchwork of tastes as our living
room walls, our adolescences sacrificed to the Jesus of lust,
the Jesus of guilt, the Jesus of our mothers, the Buddhist
tenets I studied in college, the Quaker meetings in which
he learned the language of silence and peace, the midnights
we rebelled and cursed ourselves *goddamn* into mirrors.

3

It is snowing harder now in Boston, and by chance of luck
(if there is chance or luck) we are pulled by the architecture into
the steaming mouth of one of these churches, into a sanctuary
empty except for a gathering choir and a string quartet
rehearsing behind the pulpit for a Bach concert. It is cold
out and in this warmth we decide to stay, where the moment
he and I lock arms and start toward the front of the church,
the quartet begins to play the wedding march for
absolutely no reason—and for absolutely every reason.

4

Oh, God the father, God the universe, God the snow
falling, oh god the nothingness you tell us we're right
where we're supposed to be. I do
not know where any of these ideas of you will be on this
same street one month / one week / two days from
tonight when calves are gnashed and shredded. There are
some hours I don't know what of you I believe in, or how much
or how little faith I have in human beings. But I do
know this man, this soon-to-be husband of mine, that I do
have faith in him. That for all this talk of what might be,
he has always been my love; what *is*.

FROM IAN YOUNG

24 July 2014

We spent the day in the meadow   planting
roses   tacking up eaves troughs   eating
sausage rolls   potato salad & apricots

Now in high summer the trees that surround
the meadow have dense foliage so they
shield the meadow totally from the outside world

Quite a few dragonflies around today
I thought   to be here in this enchanted place
with a beautiful beloved friend

& be at liberty & able to enjoy it.
What more could one want   I don't
want anything more than this

AN AUTUMN BOUQUET

I dream of your grandfather saying
we grow what we need. I wake

loving my own body. After
we shower, you stand behind me

at the mirror, showing
me how to steady the blade at my neck,

how to not take everything off. Before you,
the longest I'd gone without shaving was

three days, four. Now it's a week or more and
my face has grown you flowers. You lay

gifts at the base of my temples. My pride
in this garden runs from root to pit.

Soon I'll be the color of winter things,
of links in steel chains strong enough

to pull down tree and pull up skyscraper.
There'll be a cold so deep that if held long enough

against the meat of your buttocks it will scream
in burn. Then will come a moment in the whipping

snow when you allow a chest, a cry, a gentleman.
Seasons change. We prepare one another.

We grow what we need
or it grows us first.

THIS TELEPATHY IS INTRUSIVE

Ted said the telepathy between he and Sylvia was
intrusive. A year into us I understand
what he meant, the half-
joke of it and the truth in the joke.
There are days you think of running
away, not from me but from the world
and I, remembering some power
of a past life, become the air
you've no choice but to burn.
There are times I want to wallow in
the worst of myself, swallow the seed
and let the guilt of next Tuesday
grow like a weed. You appear,
gardener-husband. You
mow the lawn every
goddamn time.

ROOSTER

We bring a second dog home,
a puppy, three-months old, you
picked from the shelter. We'd agreed on
an older dog, one already trained, one who
understands his place in our world. Instead
there's this puppy in his crate the first two
nights but by the third he's sleeping
between us. I grow to love him
by the second week, when you and I
have figured out how to touch
one another again.

CLOSING THE GATES

We've struggled a little
to define where your body ends
and mine begins. To write out rules
for every situation when
rules are built to break. You say
I can play in the landfill of my mind,
be a body pressed in the ruin
of some rusted shell of a Cadillac.
You say you understand when I can't
stand myself. You say
you love me. You know I love you.

I lowered the drawbridge. I rode across
the river and felt like some sort of hero
until I didn't. Sometimes I look in
the mirror and like the way my
legs have grown desirable. Though
sooner or later, everything outside us
is nothing but blur. I think I like
what I see, all the sharp-edged monsters
who want to take a bite. Part of me wants
to let them eat me up; I don't know why.
But more of me wants to never have
you question whether I'll be home
before the moon dies another sad death.

Last night you kissed my eyelids. Do you know
you're the only person who would ever think
to do such a thing? Do you know I take
these pills to protect myself from myself?
Do you know why I hit delete this morning,
hit reset, and flushed those pills away?
Because you've given me enough
rope to hang these shirts of other boys
that never really fit, then close the door
and crawl into bed next to you.

ISHERWOOD JOURNALS

I am always on the lookout for coincidences
in dates he wrote at 34. I am 34 and mindful
how so few of us use roadmaps anymore

to get to where we think we're going. I read
your face too easily sometimes, when you want
to be left alone to battle your mood or the room

is too loud for the portraits midwifed in your brain.
I read your body like these books, always
open to things likely to flush the cheeks,

digestion of last night's dinner, tomorrow's
mortality, the sexual pull toward empty boys,
the constant questioning of treasure and worth.

How terribly insecure we all can feel. Just because
I in fact won't leave him, I have taken it
for granted he somehow knows this.

Just because
I in fact won't leave you, I have taken it
for granted you somehow know this.

I DREAM OF EMMA JEAN

I wake feeling anxious
from dreams of poor reviews
Borland, don't write backwards and
meeting my high school English teacher
at a football game   She pretends
not to remember who I am
I'm the one whose brother died
She is not impressed by one book
or the second or the third   She pretends
not to be impressed by the awards
All I want to do is thank her
but she only sees the brute of me
My husband zips my jacket
Says he's getting me
out of this stadium where
everyone is watching   We are half-
way to the anonymous street
when I notice he is cold
I give him my jacket   give him my
shirt   I turn around   begin to walk
back   Everyone is looking   I say
I've been through worse   I say
I can get through anything

THIS IS WHAT IT'S LIKE

to be a poet married to a poet. You
have to grab the good stuff first or you'll be forever
writing the same poem. Like when we read a
William Carlos Williams' interview where he struggles
for speech and train of thought, when his wife
Flossie sits in and edits his dates and protects the truth
of his stories. I say out loud I want to write a poem
of this, of these two, of their marriage, of what became
by necessity a marriage of poets (Flossie, not a poet
in practice, but in prayer: Bill turned
her notes to him into quatrains, and I
wonder if she was okay with this). My husband
laughs: *Did you just piss on this book?* He means to
mark my writing territory. To claim this subject
the same way he claimed the crow we watched
die beautiful in our neighbor's yard. We race.
How could we not, when any given touch
of hand or wrong of heart could end
up in a stranger's library? Yesterday
my husband had plum jam on his toast.
Today he made me see the face of God in my own
collarbone. These things will find their way into
our work. We're lucky. We've doubled
our odds. One of us will always write the memory.
This is just to say I don't mind when it's not me.

WHAT WE DO

I spend the morning of what would have been my father's 67th birthday on the fifth floor of the library downtown in the large window overlooking the freeway and the city skyline with my husband who never knew my father.

It's a sunny day, one of those days we always get in Arkansas in January when it's warmer than it should be after it's been colder than it should have been and we feel more alive because of it.

I have stacks of books around me, Carl Phillips' *Silverchest* and Emily Dickinson's *The Gorgeous Nothings*, but I start with Marie Howe's *What the Living Do* because I know Michael Klein adores her and when Michael Klein adores somebody the way he talks about them or writes about them makes you adore the idea of them too.

When I start with the first page I'm sitting in a chair but by the second page I've slid down to the floor with my back against the chair because that's how it feels I'm supposed to read these poems, weak-legged and hungry and tangled and messy in the sun on the rough carpet in this library.

An hour or so passes and I read the entire book, all about her platoon of a family and the life and death of her brother and how and why she loves people or maybe sometimes doesn't.

I came here to write something about my father, about the dream I had last night where I was unable to reach him by telephone. About how I knew he was there but I just couldn't get through to speak to him and how I hadn't talked to him in whatever is the dream equivalent of a really long time.

Instead I think about Marie.

About how she says her brother's death made a new way for her to live.

About Seth and I sitting in this library because my dad gave me some money to publish a book and then ten days later he was dead and I published the book and then I published another and then was invited to speak at a church about them and how that's where I met Seth.

And this morning, how we sit in the sun in the library and read poetry.

I keep reaching into Seth's study of the Dickinson book to read him lines from Marie Howe and he listens and he smiles and he nods and he doesn't get annoyed when I interrupt him maybe six or seven times. Or maybe he does get annoyed but he doesn't show it. Or maybe the lines I read out loud weave around the lines he's reading. Maybe I'm answering his questions before he asks them. Sometimes poetry works this way. Sometimes poems whisper to other poems like lovers.

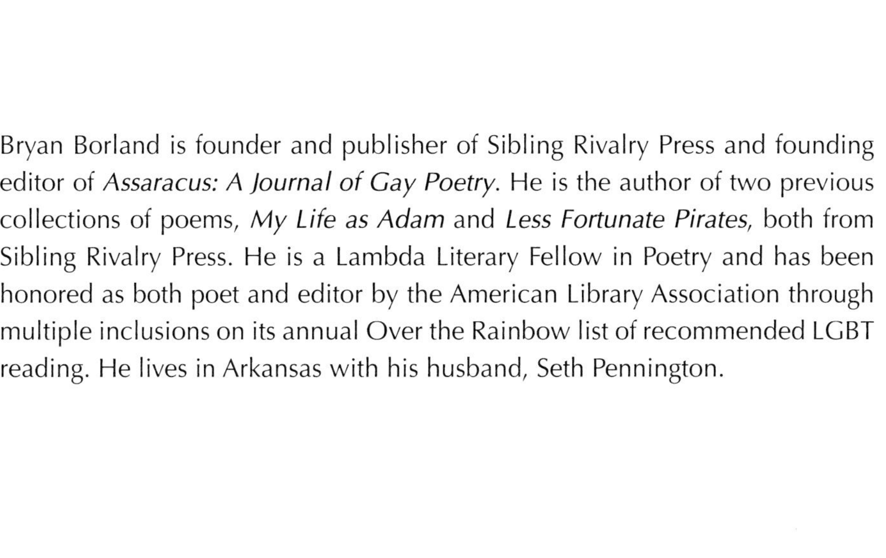

Bryan Borland is founder and publisher of Sibling Rivalry Press and founding editor of *Assaracus: A Journal of Gay Poetry*. He is the author of two previous collections of poems, *My Life as Adam* and *Less Fortunate Pirates*, both from Sibling Rivalry Press. He is a Lambda Literary Fellow in Poetry and has been honored as both poet and editor by the American Library Association through multiple inclusions on its annual Over the Rainbow list of recommended LGBT reading. He lives in Arkansas with his husband, Seth Pennington.

ACKNOWLEDGMENTS

Thank you to the editors of the journals, newspapers, websites, anthologies, and literary magazines where many of these poems first appeared (often in earlier forms and sometimes with alternate titles).

The Advocate
Satellite Passing Overhead

The Arkansas Times
Dive

Between: New Gay Poetry
The Jumpers

Chelsea Station
Easter in Your Hometown

Chiron Review
At a Bach Concert
Look Alive, Kid
The Significance of Matthew
This Telepathy Is Intrusive

Come Hear! Number 8: A Collection of Poems from the Public Reading Curated by Nathaniel A. Siegel & Regie Cabico at the 6th Annual Rainbow Book Fair
Eat the Whole World

The Gay & Lesbian Review Worldwide
Isherwood Journals
These Boys: Olive Handkerchief

Glitterwolf
Lonoke

The Good Men Project
I'll Tell Your Little Brother Years from Now
Mirror Boys

HIV Here & Now
New Drug

OCHO
An Autumn Bouquet
Communion
The Waiter, The Revolutionary, The Legislator, & The Poet

Out of Sequence: The Sonnets Remixed
Slaughter in Three Parts

RHINO
I'll Tell Your Little Brother Years from Now

Weave
These Boys: Gold Handkerchief

Velvet Mafia
These Boys: White Handkerchief

NOTES

The title "The Body Is a Damn Hard Thing to Kill" was taken from a line in the Anne Sexton poem, "The Break."

Two lines in "Communion" have been adapted and modified from their original appearance in Adrienne Rich's poem, "Ghazals: Homage to Ghalib." Original text appeared as: "The friend I can trust is the one who will let me have my death. / The rest are actors who want me to stay and further the plot."

The title "Eat the Whole World" is from a line in the Thom Gunn poem, "The Differences."

The final lines of "Friends ask us how we know this marriage is right" are from M.A. Vizsolyi's poem, "Clip Clop." This poem is in direct conversation with the poem in my previous book, "The Night I Fight with My Husband" from *Less Fortunate Pirates*. It answers the fear raised in that poem.

The title "Gold and Silver Mixed to One" is a line from the William Carlos Williams poem, "Love." "Gold and Silver Mixed to One" is for Laure-Anne Bosselaar.

The italicized portions of "Isherwood Journals" are from Christopher Isherwood's journals.

The italicized portions of "Summering with Andy Warhol" are from Andy Warhol's diaries.

"You, House Martin" is after Anne Sexton's "You, Doctor Martin." I was deep into my study of Anne Sexton when we moved to a house on Martin Street. It felt serendipitous.

Gratitude to the many helpful hands and voices along the way: Leslie Harris, Loria Taylor, Michael Klein, D. Gilson, Sarah Rawlinson, Virginia Bell, Christopher Hennessy, Ocean Vuong, Carlton Fisher, Kazim Ali, sam sax, Paul Tran, Sara Brickman, Annah Anti-Palindrome, Emily Jaeger, Ife-Chudeni Oputa, Imani Sims, Kelly McQuain, Lauren Shufran, Mat Wenzel, C. Russell Price, Nickole Brown, Jessica Jacobs, Noah Stetzer, Breana Steele, Lucas Rudd, Scott Siler, Erik Schuckers, Tina Parker, Laure-Anne Bosselaar, Marvin Moody, Mark Allen, Craig Cotter, John Cline, Ed Madden, Eric Nguyen, Donnelle McGee, Steven Sanchez, Katie Johnsonius, Anthony Lioi, Gene Mullins, Wayne Courtois-Seligman, Charles Jensen, Russell Bunge, Wynne Taillac, Liz Ahl, Collin Kelley, Noel Mariano, Eduardo C. Corral, Hugh Tipping, Denise Duhamel, Maureen Seaton, Felice Picano, Martin Regner, Philip F. Clark, Ian Young, Kirby Congdon, William Johnson, Mark Manivong, Zavé Martohardjono, William Lung, Kyle Sawyer, Tony Valenzuela, John Andrews, Will Stephenson, David Koon, Perry Brass, M.A. Vizsolyi, Paul Romero, and Jonathan Kent Adams.

Love to my Stillhouse Press family, especially to Doug and Marcos.

Love to my Sibling Rivalry Press family.

Thank you to Maya Angelou, Adrienne Rich, Anne Sexton, W. S. Merwin, Allen Ginsberg, Frank Stanford, Gwendolyn Brooks, Galway Kinnell, William Carlos Williams, Thom Gunn, Christopher Isherwood, and all the gods who come down to sing for me.

Thank you to my mother, who has never let me go one day in my life without feeling loved.

Thank you to my father, who is showing up more and more in the mirror.

Love to my blood family and my married-into family. "I'm a lucky man to count on both hands the ones I love."

Finally, to my husband, Seth Pennington. This book is a love note to you. Years ago, long before I knew you, I dreamed you were these poems.

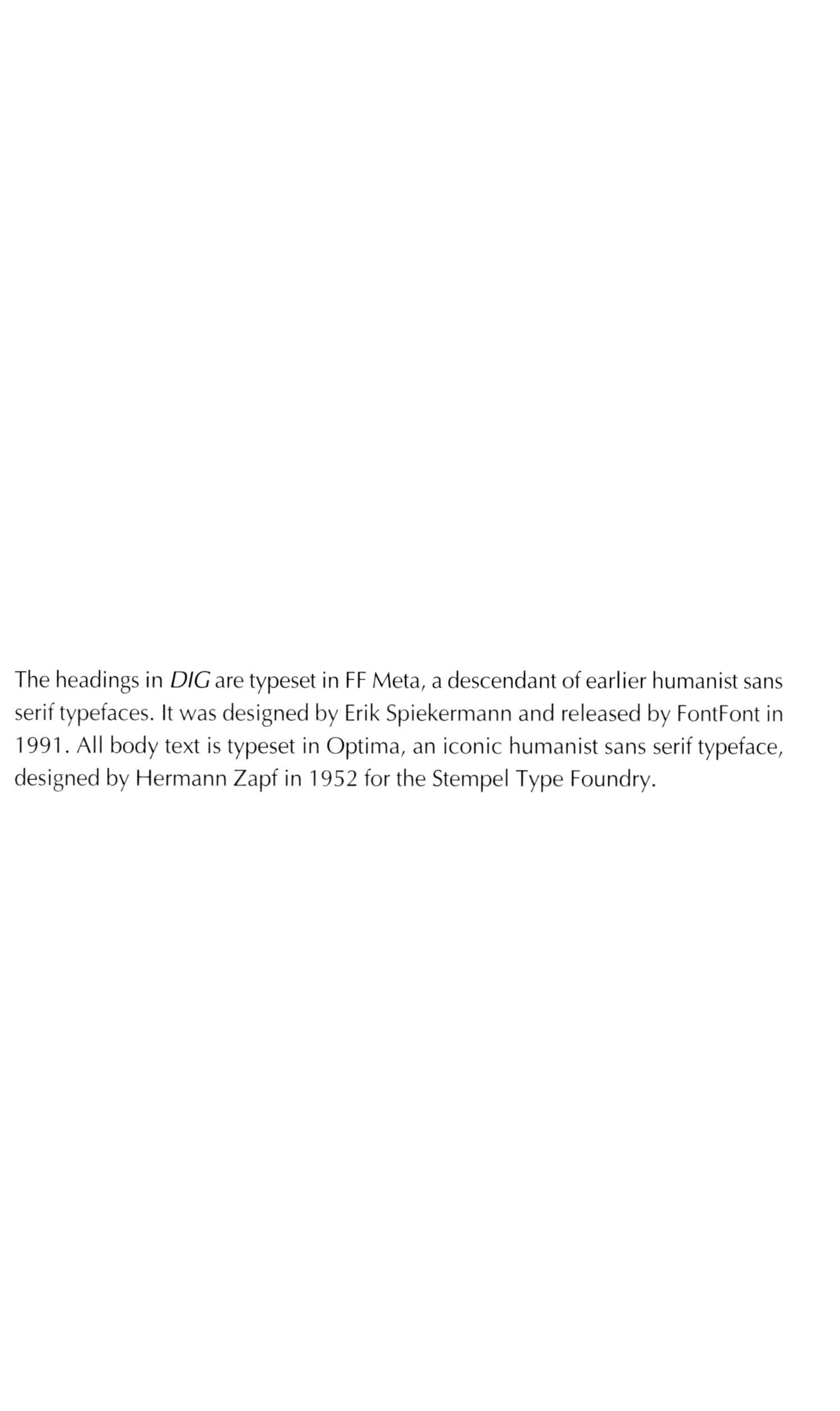

The headings in *DIG* are typeset in FF Meta, a descendant of earlier humanist sans serif typefaces. It was designed by Erik Spiekermann and released by FontFont in 1991. All body text is typeset in Optima, an iconic humanist sans serif typeface, designed by Hermann Zapf in 1952 for the Stempel Type Foundry.

This book would not have been possible without the hard work of our staff. We would like to acknowledge:

DOUGLAS J. LUMAN, MANAGING EDITOR & ART DIRECTOR
MARCOS L. MARTÍNEZ, EDITOR-IN-CHIEF
MEGHAN MCNAMARA, DIRECTOR OF MEDIA & COMMUNICATIONS
SCOTT W. BERG, EDITORIAL ADVISOR

Editors

QINGLAN WANG
BENJAMIN RADER
MELANIE TAGUE

Our Donors

ANONYMOUS
GERALD PROUT
MAZIAR GAHVARI
DALLAS HUDGENS
WAYNE B. JOHNSON
WILLIAM MILLER